It's Really More Simple Than That!

A Story About Real Life

To Chantelle
Embrace the Journey!
Namaste
Don

By
Donald Hood

All rights reserved. No part of this work may be reproduced (except in reviews) unless prior arrangement is made with the author. Besides, it would bring bad karma into your life!

Copyright © 2002-20010
By
Donald Hood

Published by
Staysail Publishing
Wheaton, IL

Cover photo: Sunset on Lake Michigan
By Donald Hood

Notes and Stuff

You have this book for a reason. You bought it, someone gave it to you or you borrowed it. However it came to you is not as important as it coming to you. Maybe it is time to read it. Maybe later. Everything is presented to us at the right time if we pay attention. It will come back around again if we don't.

I want to thank all of my many teachers, both the ones who taught me how to be and those how not to be. I thank my family, both blood related and spiritually related. I thank my teachers from both sides who have had the loving patience to keep me on track. Most importantly, my best teacher, my wife Cheri, for without her help and faith this book would not be in your hands now.

The framework of this book is somewhat autobiographical but it is by no means true in the sense of actual events. The truth is here, as it is in many texts.

Find your truth within and share that truth with others. You were brought to this text for a reason. Take what speaks to you with my blessing, and may your journey be full of life, love and light.

Namaste',
    Don

Contents

THE FIRST TIME WE MET	1
AGAIN, THE MONK	24
THE ABC'S OF LIFE	31
A LESSON IN RELIGIONS	39
SO WHAT ABOUT GOD?	58
WHO TAUGHT YOU?	74
ON THE SUBJECT OF MASTERS	82
THE CIRCLE OF LIFE	86
THE SECRETS OF LIFE	98
WHAT DO I DO NOW?	116

It's Really More Simple Than That!

It's Really More Simple Than That!

THE FIRST TIME WE MET

It was a particularly dark night the first time we met. It was late fall with a chill in the air. Everyone was busy going in their own direction wrapped up in their own little worlds. I wanted to get some more books from the library before it closed. I'd been reading everything I could get my hands on concerning spirituality. I found that the university library had a good selection, books that were much deeper than the usual stuff one could find at the local bookstore.

I pulled into the parking lot and walked over to the old building. I went right up to the top floor. In the back corner were books on religion and spirituality, philosophy and the occult. I had stumbled upon

It's Really More Simple Than That!

this section when I was up here two weeks earlier and had been wanting to get back to it ever since. There was something very familiar about this part of the library, something I couldn't put my finger on, but it felt like home.

I found my corner and nestled in with a dozen or so books sprawled around me. I had been there for about an hour and a half when I heard a voice behind me ask, "What are you looking for?" I looked up and saw a priest in his robes looking down on me.

"What are you looking for?" he asked again. This man was decidedly Italian. I figured that he must be part of the divinity school connected with the university.

"I am looking for books on religion and spirituality," I said.

It's Really More Simple Than That!

"What are you looking for?" he asked again.

"I am looking for books on the truth. Spiritual books."

"It's really more simple than that!" he said.

I glanced down at all of the books I had in my lap and on the floor. When I looked up, he was gone!

I got up and looked for him. I figured that he was probably in the next section. That was where the heavy religious books were. Most of the seminary students hang out there, although they are usually dressed more casually then this guy. The area was completely empty. This Italian fellow was probably a foreign exchange student or maybe even a professor. Either way, he was nowhere to be found.

There is a lone desk and a lone ref-

It's Really More Simple Than That!

erence librarian by the door to the stairs and elevator. This was the only way in or out. When I asked her if she had seen this Italian priest, she said no. In fact, she said that I was the only one up here for the last two hours.

This was very intriguing! How could someone get in, talk to me, and then disappear? These librarians are like hawks; nothing gets past them. In fact, you have to sign in and out because of the many rare books that are located up there. I suppose it was possible that she could have been on another part of the floor, but they are not supposed to leave their post. I could conceive of her missing him coming in or going out but not both ways! She was looking at me in a funny way and suggested that I wrap things up, as it was time to close.

I chose a couple of books that "felt

It's Really More Simple Than That!

right" and made my way out of the building. As I was walking down the stairs I clearly heard his voice in my head. "It's really more simple than that!" His voice was so clear even with the accent. Who was this man who came into my life and vanished? Maybe it was just my imagination.

I brought the books home but never got around to reading them. I got caught up in the daily grind of "up early, work hard, stay up to wind down, and sleep," only to start the whole process over again the next day. I am a cabinetmaker. I had always wanted to be one, so I took the training and here I was. The romance of making fine furniture in exotic woods drew me into the work. The reality was just making another box for someone to hang on their wall or stick in their bathroom. Sure, I was working with some nice woods but it all boiled down to the making of another box. Not very fulfilling by a

It's Really More Simple Than That!

long shot. I needed something more. What was it that I needed? I had done many things in my life. I went where I was drawn, but there was always something missing. I wanted more. More of what? I didn't know. I just knew that there was something nudging me along the way. I had tried to pay attention to this nudging. That's how I ended up on the top floor of the university library.

I never did get to those books, but I brought them back the next week and instead of going to my corner, I walked around the whole floor to see if "my priest" was there. Again, I was alone on the floor except for the sentry librarian.

I went to my corner, and there he was! Sitting in a chair at the end of the row. He must have moved the chair over from one of the tables because it had never been there before.

It's Really More Simple Than That!

"I have been waiting for you," he said.

Why was he waiting for me? What did he want?

Various fundamental religious groups have approached me and I don't have anything to say to them. It seems that all they want is to make you feel guilty for not believing exactly how they do or they create fear in you if you don't take up their cause. The "God will get you" groups.

Maybe he was part of some kind of cult that recruits lost souls from dark libraries! This didn't ring true.

There was a quality about him that I couldn't put my finger on. He had a gentle strength about him that made me feel quite comfortable even though it was disconcerting how he would seemingly appear and disappear. I wanted to ask him how he got past the sentry.

It's Really More Simple Than That!

"You want to ask me a question but it isn't really what you want to know," he said quietly. His voice was definitely Italian but completely understandable. It was almost as if he was talking only to me and nothing else existed. How did he know that I wanted to ask him anything, let alone not the question that was on my mind but something deeper?

"You said that it's more simple than that. What do you mean 'it' and 'more simple' than what?" I tried to keep my voice down so that the library sentry would not come and disturb us.

"What are you looking for?" he asked quite simply.

"What do you mean? 'What am I looking for?'" I asked.
"Inner peace, a sense of connectedness to the whole of life? Love?" he asked.

It's Really More Simple Than That!

"Yeah, I want to know all that stuff," I said.

"All that stuff, hmmm. How much time are you willing to commit to this search of yours?" he asked.

"Whatever it takes," I said without hesitation, although I was wondering what I was getting myself into.
"Are you willing to give up everything you have now to achieve this goal? All that you know now to be true?" he asked.

I looked down at the floor to weigh what he just asked of me. When I looked up, he had vanished! Again my priest had disappeared into thin air. The chair was even gone! I looked around the stacks but, of course, I could not find him. I thought about asking the old sentry librarian but thought better of it. She was already thinking that I was a little daft.

It's Really More Simple Than That!

I slowly made my way down the stairs of the old building. I did not check out any books that night. I already had plenty to think about.

What am I willing to give up to find the truth? To find inner peace? Am I ready to give up everything to have this in my life? If I do give up all this, will I still be able to live a comfortable life?

Here is where I hit a snag. Was I living a comfortable life? I worked at a job that was unfulfilling. I was divorced, not dating, no hope of seeing anyone. The last few women I did go out with were not even from the same planet. I came home to my one bedroom apartment and opened up my tin of tuna and had my dinner of tuna and Ritz crackers. One of my extravagances - Ritz Crackers. Before I met the priest at least I had books to comfort me.

It's Really More Simple Than That!

"What do I have to lose? What do I have to gain?" It was going be a tough day at work tomorrow. I thought about these things all through the day. Something was always reminding me of our talk the night before. I decided before lunch-more tuna-that I needed to go back that night and find him. After lunch, my boss came up to me and said he needed my help on an installation of cabinets. I packed up my tools and loaded them into my car and drove over to the jobsite.

I had no idea why he hired some of the people he did because it seemed that one of the shop guys always had to fix the problems created by these "jamoke's" he got so cheap. Didn't he get it that he was spending even more money getting butchers instead of craftsmen?

I looked at the crew and out of the bunch there was one with some

It's Really More Simple Than That!

promise, so I chose him and told the rest to go home. This fellow and I got more work done in that afternoon than the six of them had accomplished in the last day and a half. His name was Jim, and he had moved here recently. He wanted to be a cabinetmaker. He was a reasonable craftsman, and I told him to learn more and really get into the business. There I was telling him to get into a business that I was wishing to leave. I told Jim that I would put in a good word with the boss.

I actually enjoyed working with Jim. The clock ticked away, and we kept working. We had to finish the job to a point that the finishers could come in and do the floor and paint. Then we could come back and put up the final trim. We finished up around eight. By the time we got back to the shop and I was on the road, it was almost nine. I was thinking about working with Jim and how it got my mind off

It's Really More Simple Than That!

of the priest and his question. Out of the corner of my eye I saw a flash of red and slammed on the brakes. Around the corner screamed a fire engine and only then did I hear the piercing siren. I carefully continued on to the university.

The library stayed open until ten, so I thought I would still be able to make it. As I came to the railroad crossing, the gates came down. The switch engine slowly crossed over in front of me and had only a few cars. Good, I thought; but then just as it cleared the gate, it started to come back again and switched over to the next track. They were dropping off a boxcar to the factory on the siding down the way. Not far enough down the way because the engine sat directly in front of me. And sat directly in front of me. And still sat directly in front of me. What were they doing-unloading the car right then and there? Why was this happening? I

It's Really More Simple Than That!

needed to get to the library! I looked at my watch. It was nine-forty, and I had a mile to go before the university!

Finally, the train moved out of the way. I raced down the road praying that the cop at the speed trap was either eating donuts or asleep. As I pulled into the parking lot it was ten minutes to ten. If I could just get up there to see him for a minute...
I jumped out of the car and charged up the steps to the library. Five minutes to ten. As I got through the door, I heard the announcement, "The library will be closing in FIVE MINUTES!"
I knew the back stairs and started to charge up the seven flights to see my priest. I could feel my heart beating against my chest. I had just passed the fourth floor when I heard doors closing and locks being thrown. I picked up my pace and made it to the sixth floor. I was just about out of steam when I got to the door on

It's Really More Simple Than That!

the seventh floor. Just as my hand reached for the knob I heard the bolt slide over to lock the door. Damn!

Why? Why couldn't I talk to him for just a minute? I was trying to catch my breath when I heard a voice inside my head: "Not tonight, my friend."

I slowly made my way down the stairs and by the time I made it to the bottom, they started to turn off the lights. I surprised a couple of librarians as I pushed out through the door.
The air outside seemed to be fresher, clearer than when I went charging up those stairs. I didn't drive home right away. I walked around some and ended up at a little coffee shop where I would sometimes stop by and read. Only tonight I had nothing to read. I noticed the students around me. Some were studying; some were with dates. A few were alone like me. Except, I was different. I was not a

It's Really More Simple Than That!

student here. I came and used the library. I could check out books because I lived in the community. I had no initials after my name nor would I ever have them, not in this lifetime. I ordered a coffee and sat down in the corner. Everything seemed to be a little more in focus than before. I sat and thought about my new friend. Where did he go? Where did he stay when he wasn't surprising unsuspecting readers in dark libraries?

I drove back home to my apartment and dropped into bed. It felt as though everything had been sucked out of me. I was completely drained. What was I willing to give up to find inner peace? Didn't know, didn't care. I fell asleep.

I heard a noise at the door and got up. I was a little wobbly and didn't know what time it was. I opened the door and found myself standing on the edge of a cliff. The mountains

It's Really More Simple Than That!

across the way were beautiful and rose up into the clouds. It was cold-fresh, really. I was pleasantly surprised that I had no fear. There I was standing on a cliff, God knows how high, barefoot and without as much as a jacket. The odd thing was that I never questioned why I was on this cliff.

I looked across the way and saw an old man. He was short and dressed in monk's robes. He was sitting cross-legged and a staff leaned up next to him. He was watching me with a slight smile on his face. This little man on the side of a frozen mountain seemed as content as most people would be on a sunny beach. He just sat watching me. A strange feeling came over me. Strange, because I was getting warmer. A sense of calm I had never felt before washed over me. He was just watching me, and I was watching him. As we were watching each other, I felt that he was

It's Really More Simple Than That!

getting closer. Then, I realized I was getting closer to him. I was floating across the valley! I looked down and could see the whole valley. It was beautiful! There were lush gardens, and I could make out animals and people tending their crops. When I looked back up at the little man I heard, or rather felt him say, "How much?" Just then, he disappeared, and I began to fall.

When I woke up, I was back in my bed covered in sweat. "What the hell was that!?" I shouted out to no one in particular. I knew it was just a dream, and I knew I didn't really open my door to a range of mountains. There was no little monk. But why did I have his staff in my room? I fell back to sleep.

I woke up to my alarm, which was particularly annoying, the next morning. I got up and went through my morning ritual and ran out the door

It's Really More Simple Than That!

buttoning my shirt as I went. I got to the shop just in time. We were having a meeting about how we needed to increase our production. The manager droned on for a while. We all looked concerned and then nodded and smiled at the appropriate times. Finally, we got back to work and I could contemplate what happened to me the night before. Wait until I tell the priest what happened, I thought. He probably already knows. This was probably his idea in the first place.

The boss came over and thanked me for getting things straightened out over on the jobsite. He asked why I let the others go. I told him that out of the whole bunch, Jim was the only one who knew what was going on. He then asked me if I wanted to be the foreman out in the field and run all the jobsites. It would mean a raise and more benefits. I told him I would think about it.

It's Really More Simple Than That!

At the end of the day I got out of there as soon as I could. I didn't want the boss to come find me for "another opportunity." On my way to the library I noticed that I seemed to be sailing along faster than normal but I wasn't speeding. All the traffic was clear and there was no train in sight at the crossing. I even found a place in the lot to park up front. That never happens!

I went up to the seventh floor to look for my priest. I took the elevator this time. He was waiting for me. He was sitting there as casually as a man without a care in the world.
"Welcome back," he said, "I missed you last night."

"I got up to the door, and the librarian locked it just as I got there!"

"No she didn't, that was me," he replied simply.

It's Really More Simple Than That!

"What do you mean that was you?" I asked. "Why didn't you let me in?

"You were late," he said quietly.
"But, I tried to get here. I had to fix my boss' goof-up with bad employees; I almost got creamed by a fire engine and then the train ..." I protested. He was smiling. I realized that it did not make any difference. I was late, and I knew it.
"Where do we go from here?" I asked.

"Where do you want to go?" he asked. "This is real life, the possibilities are endless! How much time do you have? Careful--it's a trick question."
What does he mean, "a trick question?" I thought. "The library closes in three hours," I said.

"And is that all the time you have, just three hours?"

He asked it in a way that made me

It's Really More Simple Than That!

think I may not have thought this through exactly right. What was he getting at? "Well, I have more, but we have only three hours here in the library," I said with some confidence.

"Then what happens?" he asked.

"Uh, the library closes, and we split for the night," I said tentatively.

"So, you think that we are limited to just being in the library? To just meet and then go our separate ways?"

He sounded almost indignant. I was a little flustered. It seemed that whatever answer I gave it would not be what he wanted. What did he want? He was the elusive one. Did he want to come home with me? I didn't think I am ready for a roommate again. He does seem harmless, but you never know.

Although, he did have this sense

It's Really More Simple Than That!

about him that seemed to embody peace. A gentle strength.

It's Really More Simple Than That!

AGAIN, THE MONK

When I came back to the library the priest was waiting for me out in front.

"Let's go!" he said.

The priest took off running down the street. No one seemed to notice this tall man with flowing robes flying by them. He never bumped into anyone even though the sidewalk was crowded. I did my best to keep up with him but it was hard. All of a sudden he darted down the steps to the subway. Of course he did not have to pay as he glided past the turnstiles. I stopped to pay the fare and looked up as he darted down the platform. I tried to keep up, but he was already at the end when my foot reached the platform.

It's Really More Simple Than That!

He got to the end of the platform and slipped through the door. I got to the door just as the express train raced through the station. When I was on the other side, I realized that I was at the edge of the cliff again facing the monk sitting on the side of the mountain. How does he do this, I wondered?

He was sitting in the lotus position on this ledge just as easy as one sits at the lunch counter. His eyes were half closed, and he asked me how long had I been waiting?

I said that we only just arrived. He said that that's not what he meant.

Waiting for what? I thought.

He asked again, "How long have you been waiting?"

I finally realized that he meant how long had I been waiting to realize my

It's Really More Simple Than That!

spiritual path. "Since I can remember," I said. Whew, that was easy.

He looked up at me and smiled. "Is that a long time?" he asked.
Oh-oh, trick question again. "I think so," I replied.

I turned to the priest to see if I had done okay, but he was gone. It was just the old monk and me. I knelt down in front of him and was quiet for a while. I was thinking to myself that if I didn't speak up we would just be sitting for a long time. Maybe that was the point: to sit and be quiet.

We sat…for a long time. At least it seemed so.

Finally, he asked, "What are you looking for?"

"The simplicity of life," I replied. "Why do you come all the way up here to find out that? Can you not

It's Really More Simple Than That!

find that wherever you are?"

"I know that I am supposed to. But it doesn't come that easy."
"Who said it was easy?"
"Doesn't the word simplicity imply easy?" I asked.

"Simple has nothing to do with easy. Simple means without complications. It means that when you look, you see clearly."

He was sitting contentedly with his eyes half open. "How do you like your new friend?" he asked.

"He seems very interesting," I said.

"Just interesting? What do you want from him?" he asked.
"I don't know. He said that finding the truth was simple."
"No he didn't. He said that the truth was simple, not the finding of it."

It's Really More Simple Than That!

"What's the difference?" I asked.

"Sometimes the path we choose is complicated."

"Why does it have to be complicated?"
"I did not say it had to be complicated. I said that sometimes we choose a path that is complicated."

"Why would anyone choose a complicated path?"

"How is your path?" was all he replied.

I stood and looked down at my feet. I knew he had me. Everything I had tried had not worked out very well, and here I was on the edge of a cliff talking to a monk. When I looked up, he was standing in front of me, inches from my face.

"What is your commitment to this

It's Really More Simple Than That!

path you have chosen?" He was moving closer to me as I was stepping back. He was in my face, gentle but in my face. What did he want of me?

"I want- no-I need to know the truth."

"Is that all?" he said. He moved closer. I nodded and edged back. I was on the edge of the cliff. I was afraid. Afraid of him. Afraid of this path. Afraid of falling to my death.

He touched his forehead to mine and said, "You already know the truth."

When he pulled back, I felt as though I was falling. I screamed out, but there was no sound. Everything rushed past me at increasing speed, and I braced myself for the inevitable crushing death.

I shot up out of my bed, drenched in sweat and scared to death. What am

It's Really More Simple Than That!

I doing? Where is all this taking me? I am so tired.

It's Really More Simple Than That!

THE ABC'S OF LIFE

I was back in the library with the priest and we were tucked back in the corner of the library.

"Today we are going to learn the 'ABC's of Life,'" he said.

"ABC's?" I asked.

"Yes, without these, we would die," he stated in his all knowing tone.

"Okay, what are they?" I asked this knowing that it would be something pretty obvious once he explained it to me. He always started out simple and then got more complicated before we came back to simple again.

"Always Breathe Continuously," he said with a sweeping gesture as if to make it more important.

It's Really More Simple Than That!

"That's it? That can't be it. Don't we just do it all the time anyway?" I thought he must have been joking.

"Wait a minute. Let's do this first." He touched my head, and we were in the middle of the expressway! Not in a car- just standing in the middle on the line. I started to scream out, and he stopped me. My heart was racing and I felt sweat rolling down my body. He told me to calm down; we were not going to get hurt. With the cars were whizzing past so closely, I knew we were doomed. He squeezed my head and in a flash, we were back at the library! I was covered in sweat, but I was safe.

"Whew! That was a close one! Why did you do that, are you crazy?"

"Why did you stop breathing when we were out on the expressway?" was all he asked.
"Stop breathing? I didn't stop

It's Really More Simple Than That!

breathing! That was crazy! You never know what those drivers will do when you're in a car, but to be out in the middle of the road like that means that you are just a target!" I was all but shouting at him, and I was breathing hard.

"Why are you breathing so hard now?" he asked.

"Because I am upset! That's why. That was the most reckless thing you have ever done with me!"

"You're upset."

"Damn right I'm upset! I don't think this whole teacher/student thing is going to work out." I felt like I was going to explode.

"Why aren't you breathing now?" He put his hand on my head; again we floated in some huge body of water. I could not even tell which way was up.

It's Really More Simple Than That!

He smiled at me. Now I really felt like I was going to explode. He took my hand and gave it a little jerk up and-flash-we were back in the library.

I gulped in a big breath of air and noticed where we were and that our clothes were already dry. "Oh," I said. "This whole thing was about the breath, right?"

"So you might think the breath might be important?" he asked. "Of course you could not breathe when you were in the ocean, but why couldn't you breathe when we were on the expressway?"

"I was afraid," was all I said.

"So fear kept you from breathing?" he asked, smiling that annoying smile of his.
"Yes, fear! I was afraid that we were going to get creamed out there!" I was showing frustration again.

It's Really More Simple Than That!

"But there was air to breathe. Why did you choose not to do so?" Again with that annoying smile.

"I had other things on my mind, okay?" I was shouting again.

"Other things were more important than the breath?" he asked. "What could be more important than the breath?"

He had me there, I thought. I could feel my body tense when I got upset or scared. But what could I do about it?

"Sit!" he said all of a sudden. "I will teach you how to breathe."

He had me sit down with my back straight and my face looking forward. "Now start counting, at a moderate pace, one… two… three… four… one… two… three… four… and so on."

It's Really More Simple Than That!

I started counting and found by the second set of numbers, I was out of breath. He told me to slow down and breathe in on the one-two count and out on the three-four count. I did and it seemed very comfortable but controlled. I thought breathing was supposed to be natural.

"It is," he said, reading my mind. "Just keep practicing."

"Now visualize the breath coming up the back of your spine and down your front. This creates a complete circle and will help your flow of energy."

I was doing as he instructed and I was feeling better. I felt more awake. My muscles were even beginning to relax; I could feel my shoulders beginning to drop. This was pretty neat stuff, but why count only to four; why not keep going? I thought.

It's Really More Simple Than That!

"Because you need to keep your focus on the breath not on the counting." He had read my mind again. "The count is only to help you maintain the rhythm. You will get to a point where the numbers will just drift away."

"This sounds a lot like meditation," I said.

"That's exactly what it is. Meditation will train you to breathe correctly. You may even find other benefits as well…if you pay attention."
"But I can't meditate," I protested. "I start out like the teachers say, but there is too much noise in my head, and besides, they say that it takes years to do it right. What's the point?"

"The point is that it is really more simple than that," he explained. "Many people make things out to be more difficult than necessary. Many

It's Really More Simple Than That!

'teachers' want to hold onto the 'secrets' and make it out to be hard to do. Then there are those who believe that if it is not hard to do, it isn't worth doing. We don't see the essence of the practice. The noise in your head, for instance, is going to be coming in no matter what. If you try to keep the door closed to these thoughts, your focus will be on the door and not the meditation. The idea is to let it come in and then go right out. Just like watching a train at the crossing. You've zoned out watching the cars go by, so you know what it is like already. Anything that is important will be there when you get done with the meditation. Return to the count, and keep the breath."

It's Really More Simple Than That!

A LESSON IN RELIGIONS

This time, I met him in the park by the library. He seemed to like the trees and fresh air. We never discussed this; I just knew it by the way he looked so at peace when we were in a natural setting. What was the lesson for today, I thought?

"Good afternoon," he said.

"Good afternoon," I said. "What is it for today?"

"A lesson in religions," he said matter-of-factly.

"All of them?" I said jokingly.

"Yes!" And we were off down the path that went deeper into the park. It was always hard to follow him. His pace was always a bit faster then

It's Really More Simple Than That!

mine. I sped up, and he would speed up. This kept my focus on him rather than on where we were. He almost glided along, robes flowing in the breeze as he sped down the path.

All the while that I was trying to keep up with him, I was thinking, "how are we going to learn about all of the world religions in one afternoon?" He did some incredible things with time. I knew today would be interesting.

I was lost in thought and I lost him. One minute I was watching his flowing robes and the next minute, he was gone! I charged down the path that we were going on and then back again to take another that he might have gone down. I looked around and noticed that there were many paths from this point. I was at an intersection! There were several choices and they all seemed pretty equal for the most part.

It's Really More Simple Than That!

A moment of panic set in, but I pushed it back. I remembered my breathing and I realized that I had a choice. I could choose any one of the paths and walk it to find my friend. Which one should I take? I wondered.

They all looked the same. I looked down each of the paths and saw that they all took a turn a short way down. I started down one of the paths and soon found that beyond the turn, the path was very rocky. I doubted that he had come down this way, but something compelled me to continue.

Further down the path, I found my way back onto the street. Although for some reason I didn't recognize this part of town. Right in front of me stood a religious bookstore. It said "religious" but when I went inside, it only touted one religion. I thought they should have mentioned that on the outside.

It's Really More Simple Than That!

I found it interesting that the nature of the store was far less spiritual than I had expected. The shoppers all rushed around to get their items and did not pay any attention to each other. I looked around and saw that there were several books about various tragedies and how the author's religion helped them through the ordeal. They were grouped together by their particular tragedy. There were shelves and shelves of religious icons displayed tastefully along with the appropriate price tags. Also, there were all shapes and sizes and colors of their main book. I found it interesting that it almost gave the illusion of different information. It was an example of marketing at its finest. There were even bins in the middle of the aisle offering religious icon refrigerator magnets at three for a dollar. The whole store seemed to be on sale.

It's Really More Simple Than That!

The clerks in the store were far from friendly, unless they could sell you more stuff. I got the feeling that there was something else that they thought was more important than the religion that they were touting. I asked a young man if they carried any books of prayers and meditation. He gave me a look like I said something that made him uncomfortable. He thought for a moment and said that he thought maybe there might be some in the corner, if they had any at all, and then turned away.

I went over to the corner and found a small selection of books of prayer collections. The books were all placed low on the shelf and were a little dusty.

I felt more comfortable here than any other place in the store. I looked over a few of the books and thought they were pretty good. Why didn't they have them in a better place?

It's Really More Simple Than That!

I realized that I was taking too much time with this distraction. I needed to be looking for my priest so we could start my lesson. I walked out of the store and returned to the woods. I thought that maybe the priest would have ventured back to see what was taking me so long.

I went back in the way I came and after going about a hundred yards; I discovered that I was in another part of the forest. Standing in front of me was a high gate for some kind of compound. There were two young people at the gate that were being let in, so I joined them and walked in.

I looked back and two guards closed the gate and locked it. That made me somewhat nervous. I looked around and saw a very large white building surrounded by several smaller buildings. I thought it strange that none of the buildings had any windows. Just then, someone said, "Hello, I'm

It's Really More Simple Than That!

Tad, welcome to our church." We walked along a manicured path to the very large white building. I was escorted by a young man who had a crew cut and was dressed way "too perfect." Everything about this place felt odd-plastic in a way.

Just then, the young man introduced me to a woman who was dressed very similarly. She greeted me and said, "Hello, my name is Ann. It is time to go inside for our lesson."

There was quite a crowd inside. The sanctuary was completely white. White carpeting, white walls, white pews; everywhere I looked there was an absence of color. Except for the people, but they all looked pretty much alike too. This all felt kind of weird.

Music filled the place and the lights began to change. The light focused on the altar and grew brighter. It

It's Really More Simple Than That!

seemed that all the light that had been in the room was focused onto the altar. The music grew louder and out from some kind of secret door behind the altar stepped what I took to be the leader of the group. He was dressed in all white, and he almost glowed with all the light that shined on him. There was a sense of awe that went through the room.

"That man is called Jewel, and he is the chosen one," Ann said in a hushed tone. Chosen by whom, I thought to myself?

Everyone bowed his or her head, and Jewel started to speak. I could tell that his voice was enhanced by the sound system. It was deep and resonant. Maybe he was supposed to sound like God.

"You are the chosen people! God has called me here to help you reach above the crowd of unbelievers who

It's Really More Simple Than That!

wallow in their sin and misery! Follow the Teachings and you will be free! Do as I say, and you will be saved!"

Everything he said had an exclamation point on the end. He droned on and on. Finally, we were supposed to sing from a small red book about the joys of following "The Path." I thought this would be a good time to find a bathroom. I tried to excuse myself, but a strong hand gripped my arm. "We must stay until the service is finished." Tad was on my left with the iron grip. He smiled. Everyone smiled for that matter. Not the smile that says that you are happy or that you want the other person to feel safe. It was more of a mask-like, plastic smile. I was feeling uncomfortable. I felt very claustrophobic as they all droned on and on with the song. "How many verses can a song have?" I thought.

It's Really More Simple Than That!

Jewel said some final words and he went back into his hideaway behind the altar. The lights changed, and we were able to move about. I asked about the bathroom because by this time I really did have to go. Tad offered to take me. I knew by the way he offered that it was not a choice.

He took me down a long passage to the men's room and I did my business.

No window in here either, I thought. What's wrong with a few windows? That's when I noticed the air. It had a scent to it, not because of where I was; it was throughout the whole building-at least the parts that I had been in. It was a sweet smell, nice, kind of a spice.

When I came out, I asked Tad about the scent, and he said, "Jewel says that the outside air is bad for us to breathe so the air inside is filtered and treated in a way to help us feel

It's Really More Simple Than That!

more free." He was smiling that plastic smile that they all had. I had to admit that the air did smell good, but something didn't seem quite right.

He walked me back to the front part of the church where they were serving refreshments. I noticed a man who was watching me closely. He reached for one of the drinks that they were serving and his coat opened to reveal a holstered gun.

I turned to Tad and asked, "Is that man a cop?"
"Oh no," he said, "He is one our security men. Jewel says that we must be very careful because some people don't understand The Path."

"What is The Path?" I asked.
"Weren't you paying attention to Jewel's message? The Path gives us the Teachings to set us free." He said this with his plastic smile.

It's Really More Simple Than That!

I was going to ask him what the Teachings were about, but something told me to just stay quiet until I could get out of there. I was offered a drink. I accepted it graciously, but I secretly dumped it into a plant by the door. I started walking out and Tad came up and gripped my arm again in his "I'm really your friend" manner.

"You don't want to leave now, do you?"
That is exactly what I wanted.

"I need to get back, I have a sick friend who is expecting me, I've stayed too long already, thank you for sharing your hospitality with me, I'll call later sometime, bye." I was pulling him toward the gate as I said all this. The guard at the gate looked at me, then at Tad. Tad gave a nod to the guard and he unlocked the gate. As soon as I got through, it was slammed shut and locked. As I was walking down the path, I looked back

It's Really More Simple Than That!

and saw Tad still smiling through the bars.

This was a very strange day. I walked back down the path and came to another bend. In the distance I saw another compound. This one, however, looked more inviting. The fence and gate were made of wood. There was an old man at the gate and he quietly welcomed me into the open area. It was very green, lush and well cared for. He asked me if I came to meditate.

"Yes," I said. After all, the priest had taught me how to do it right. I figured I could fit in for a while.

"Please change your clothes here in this building." The old man pointed to a small building with lockers with robes and places to hang our street clothes. I quietly changed and came back out to meet him. He walked me over to another building with a large room with open sides. He put his fin-

It's Really More Simple Than That!

ger to his lips for me to be quiet and showed me where to sit.

I slipped in quietly next to a man who seemed to be in his fifties. We sat and breathed and I felt very relaxed and yet full of energy. We sat there for maybe an hour or so before there was a sound of a gong and it was time for a break.

"You were doing very well in there," said a voice from behind. "You must have been studying meditation for a very long time." He was the teacher. "Actually, I just learned how to breathe last week."

"Impossible!" He seemed angry that I would take him for a fool and lie to the great teacher. "It would take a student many years to become as proficient as you."

I did not know whether I should say thank you or feel bad because I

It's Really More Simple Than That!

caught on so quickly. I must have had a better teacher. I said nothing. I only bowed my head. He seemed to like that and moved on, but I saw him talking to the old man who let me in at the gate.

The man I was sitting next to in the meditation room came over to me and started to ask me questions. He said he had been practicing for seventeen years and still didn't get it right. I told him to stop practicing and just do it! Just then the gong sounded and everyone was asked back in for the next session. That is, everyone except me. I was shown the door.

Again, I started down the path. I had just about given up on finding my priest when I came around another bend and found a man in his thirties sitting by a small stream. I was drawn by his gentle strength and peace that surrounded him. He turned as I came

It's Really More Simple Than That!

up to him. I was going to ask him if he saw my priest. Before I opened my mouth he said that he has been waiting for me.

"How could you be waiting for me? I just happened to take this path."

"Did you?" he asked.

"Did I what?"

"Just happen to take this path." He rose and stretched out his hands to greet me.

Something made me feel that I had met this man before. I knew him. I didn't know how I knew him, I just did.

"You will find your friend soon," he said.

"How do you know that I am looking for anyone?" I asked. He took hold of both of my hands. They were

It's Really More Simple Than That!

soft, strong and gentle. I felt a sense a peace as he touched me.

"I know things."

"What kind of things?" I asked.

"I know that you are looking for the truth. I know that it is more simple than most make it out to be. And that love is the most important aspect of all things."

"You sound like my teacher."

"Your priest, as you call him."

"How do you know him?" I asked.

"He was my student."

"Your student?"

"Does that surprise you?"

It's Really More Simple Than That!

"Yes, it does, because he must be thirty years older than you," I said.

"Yes, it does appear that that is true but you can't always believe in what you see."

"How do you mean?" I asked.

"Before you, you think you see a man in his thirties, but you have no idea when I was born do you?"

"No, I don't, but aren't you in your thirties?" He smiled that same smile that the monk and priest have. The one that means that I should know something so obvious, but I don't.

"If I looked older would it be more believable that your priest was my student?" he asked, "Haven't you taught him anything yet?"
"No, I don't think I have anything to teach him," I replied.

It's Really More Simple Than That!

"Maybe you should start paying more attention!" He was looking straight into my eyes as if he were looking into my very soul. One might think that it would spook me, but instead, it gave me such a sense of inner peace. I had never felt this kind of peace before.

"What are you feeling right now?" he asked as he brought his hands up to each side of my head.

"Incredible peace and strength!" It was as if he was pouring all of the power and love of the universe into me. I felt lighter, freer, simple and a profound sense of peace.
Then an odd thing happened. I was feeling as if I was sending the love back to him! I wasn't trying to do anything, just letting him hold my head in his hands.

Still looking into my eyes, he simply said, "Remember, just remember."

It's Really More Simple Than That!

SO WHAT ABOUT GOD?

I was working on another box today and thinking about my priest. He was always talking about how "God this" or "God that" and that there was only one God. With all the trouble in other countries, how could there be only one? Wouldn't the conflicts have worked themselves out by now? And if there is only one, why hasn't He done something about all of this?

"So, what about God?" I asked as soon as I saw him in our library corner. He was perched on his chair as if he had been waiting all day just for me to show up. Maybe he had.

"What do you mean?"

"Why is your God better than anyone else's?" I wanted to know.

It's Really More Simple Than That!

"I never said that," he said, as calm as could be.

"Then why do you sound like it?"

"I talk with the passion of the Divine inside me. When we remember who we really are, then we can speak with that passion." There was a clarity in his eyes that shone deeply past his many years.

Still not satisfied I said, "Then you imply that your God is better."

"I'm not implying anything. Besides, it's not possible." And he crossed his arms.

"What isn't?" I was beginning to get confused.

"That my God is better that anyone else's."

"But you speak as if he is."

It's Really More Simple Than That!

"No, I speak with all the passion that is due our creator."
I was even more confused now. "But, what about all the other Gods?"

"What other Gods?"

"The other Gods of all the other religions!" I said, raising my voice.

"There are no 'other Gods,'" he replied calmly.
"See, that's just what I'm talking about. You make out that your God is better! Boy, you frustrate me!" I was shouting now.
"You'd better lower your voice or the nice librarian will ask you to leave."

I calmed down, but I still wanted to know. "Okay, okay, but how can you say there are no other Gods? What about the other guys?"

"What other guys are you talking about? Are we not all children of God?"

It's Really More Simple Than That!

"Yes..." He was about to launch into one of his explanations that would show me that I should have known this already.

"Then, if we are all children of God, doesn't it make sense that we all have the same parent?"

"Yes, but not everyone believes the same way you do," I said thinking that he should be aware of that little fact.

"Of course not, that's free will."

"Then how can there be only one God?" I was still confused.

"It's very much like a family."

"How so?" I ask.

"Say you belong to a large family. Lots of children. Some of those children will always accept the love

It's Really More Simple Than That!

and guidance of the parents and reflect that love to others. Some will be pretty neutral about the whole experience. Some will retaliate and disavow their parents and act out their fears. They will even say that their parents are dead. Each will describe their parents in completely different terms, yet the parents are the same." Then, leaning forward in his chair he added, "There are some children who will even go looking for other parent figures but it doesn't change the fact that they are the children of the first parents."

"What happened to free will?"

"It's always there. We can either accept free will or ignore it."

"So, we can choose another path and a different God – gotcha!" I had him now.

"What do you mean 'gotcha?' Here I thought you were beginning to un-

It's Really More Simple Than That!

derstand." He leaned back in the chair, looking disappointed.

Things were rolling now; it was coming together. "I am! You said that we have free will to choose our path. We can choose another 'parent' if we want."

"But they are not our real parent," he replied calmly, but looking like he had to start from the beginning.

"But other parents do exist don't they?" I was still thinking I had it figured out.

"Yes, but…"

"Gotcha!"

"You might want to use that word more judiciously. The family analogy may be somewhat imperfect when explaining a dynamic involving an omnipotent being. Please forgive me." He bowed his head for effect.

It's Really More Simple Than That!

"I don't 'gotcha', do I?"

He stood up, looked me in the eye and smiled. "No, but your passion is rising and that is good."

"What good is my passion if I'm wrong?"

"You're not wrong. Passion awakes the true person within. Look to the love and fear, and see where the love lies." I could feel the energy flowing through him.

"But what if my passion is so strong that I express it in violent terms for instance?"

"True passion, like true love, unconditional love, comes from God. Violence, at any level, is an act of fear. Do you think that if you were to tap into your true passion that you would be able to act in fear?"

It's Really More Simple Than That!

"Well, no, I wouldn't, but what about the zealots in our world?"

"They're acting in fear," he said as he sat back down in his chair.

"But they don't know that, right?"

"Surprisingly, most of them do and are afraid that their followers might find out. That is why they make so much noise."

"So the noisy ones are the ones acting in fear?"

"Pretty much. Look at all the leaders that you know, now and in the past. When you look at them from the perspective of love and fear, you will find this to be true."

"But some leaders that are truly passionate are loud."

"It is good to get fired up and share that passion with others. But look to

It's Really More Simple Than That!

what they say and do. Love or fear? Loud or noisy? It all boils down to love and fear."

I pulled up a chair and sat in front of him and said, "Let's get back to the God thing."

"All right, 'the God thing,'" he said with a smile.

"Are you saying that all of the Gods that the different religions have are the same guy?"

"Well, first of all, God does not have gender and yet embraces all gender. We are dealing with the omnipotent being. All things to all people, the alpha and omega, and so on. Just like the children of parents on this plane, each of us sees God in their own perspective, their own reality. This reality is shaped by their experience and colored by their past lives."
"So, one who had many lives in a

It's Really More Simple Than That!

spiritual dynamic will find this life easier than one who has had many fear-based lives."

"Probably."

"Probably? Isn't that the law of karma?"

"Yes and no. The law of karma is a law of nature. Nature is always working to maintain balance. But, in real life, humans in particular, we have free will. Free will allows us to choose the kind of lessons that we want in our next life. And that same free will allows us to choose if we want to work on them when we get here."

"That sounds complicated," I said.
"It's not really. Remember, it all boils down to love and fear and the illusion of that fear and free will."

"That sounds too simple."
"It is simple. It's not always easy. I

It's Really More Simple Than That!

never said that life was easy. Not much of a lesson if it were easy."

"Why can't we have an easy life?"

"We can, if we want. Some do choose to have an easy one for a change. But most people choose one that challenges them in some way. Usually the ones who are having the hardest time are the ones who have chosen an overload of 'coursework' for this lifetime."

"That explains why some people seem to be overwhelmed with their life and find it hard to go on," I said.

"Exactly. It does not mean that they are any smarter or dumber than the next person. It just means that they took on more than they could really handle. Sometimes it is hard to watch our brothers and sisters go through such a hard time."

It's Really More Simple Than That!

"Aren't there guides to help us choose what we come in with?" I ask.

"Yes, but it is still our choice and maybe part of the lesson is to understand how much we can or cannot do, in a lifetime."

"But, what about all the guides and angels that we are supposed to have; where are they in all of this? How come they don't step in and help out when we run into trouble?"

"They will, if we ask. We need to let them know that we would like them to help and be open to accept their help when it is offered. They are very patient and will wait for us. It is always our choice. There are some cases where they are allowed to step in at a critical time. Some of those are the miracles that you hear about. It is a fine line. They are there to help but not intervene."

"So, it is still about free choice and

It's Really More Simple Than That!

love and fear, right? So, what about the god thing?"

Just then the librarian came around the corner, startled that I was still there. "The library is closed, you will have to leave, now!" I turned to see my priest and he had vanished, of course.

On the way home I kept thinking about our talk. If there is only one god then why do we have to have all of this violence about whose god is better? How could it possibly serve the "big picture?"

I pulled into a gas station to pick up a gallon of milk and as I got out of my car, a guy came running out of the store and demanded my keys. It all happened so fast. I gave him my keys, and he knocked me in the head, and as I fell I saw him reaching for my car. The next thing I knew, I was floating and everything was a blur.

It's Really More Simple Than That!

I found myself on the top of a high mountain. Across the way, I saw my monk smiling up at me. Just then, I lost my balance and began to slide down the mountainside. I picked up momentum right away; it seemed like I was flying down the mountain. The white snow was cold and icy against my skin. About a third of the way down I came to an outcropping and was thrown into the air and fell even faster. What the hell is going on? I thought.

Everything turned white and I could not tell which way was up or down. It was as if I were floating; there was no gravity. Then I began hearing words in my head and images surrounding me spinning faster and faster. Jehovah, Allah, Krishna, Sadai, Theos, Elah, Shiva, Vishnu, Elohim, images and sounds going around so fast they were becoming a blur. Then the images all blended into one, and I heard the sound of "Om" com-

It's Really More Simple Than That!

ing deep from within my very being. There was a pulsing white light that enveloped me, and I heard a clear voice within say, "I am all, I am one." "We are all one"

"I am here"

I thought, what does it mean to be here? In the moment? In the now? When we get the message, "I am here," what are we hearing?"

Then I saw in front of me the words:
I = singular, one
Am = state of being, present tense, eternal
Here = a place, universal

Finally, I get it!

"I am here," means that the One is always present. When we hear this message we hear it inside of ourselves. This means that the One is inside, always. As we hear and say it

It's Really More Simple Than That!

to ourselves we are also acknowledging that we also are One and here and in the perfect state of being. Once we begin to accept this charge from our Creator that we were and are created in His image then we can move forward on our/His path.

I shot upright in a hospital bed. I looked around, and there was my priest sitting on the windowsill smiling at me.

He said "They admitted you as 'John Doe' because they could not find any identification on you. By the way, here's your wallet and your car is parked outside."

"What did you do to me this time?" I said.

"Nothing, although I did get some help from your monk friend," he grinned. "So, what about this 'god thing?'"

It's Really More Simple Than That!

WHO TAUGHT YOU?

The priest and I were sitting quietly in the park across from the library when I asked him, "Who taught you about all this stuff?"

"One night as I was working on my texts, a light came into the room. I was engrossed in my text and I assumed that it was one of the other monks who had entered without knocking.

"When I looked up, I saw a smallish man dressed in maroon and gold monk robes. I was startled because I never met anyone like this before.

"I was, like you, struggling for the truth. I knew there must be something more to the truth than what we were doing. We seemed to be doing all of the right things according to

It's Really More Simple Than That!

our doctrines, religiously, but there was an emptiness in my heart. Something was missing.

"I asked him how he got in and where he came from. He said that he knew that I was looking for the truth and so he thought he could give me some help. I asked him how he knew that and he just smiled.

'What are you looking for?' he said.

"I am looking for a way to bring the truth to the people, so they can look to us or themselves and find a sense of inner peace. I want to know what the truth is about life. What the truth is about who we really are.

'It's really more simple than that,' he said.

"'What?' I said, and bent to my scroll to write that down, and when I looked up, he was gone.
"I looked for him. I walked the whole

It's Really More Simple Than That!

monastery. I was afraid to ask anyone if they saw him because they might think me crazy. There was something very strange and yet very special about this little man.

"That was my first encounter and by no means my last. He came and went for the next several months. He had been a Tibetan monk and died a long time before he came to see me. He told me how he had been the right-hand guard to Genghis Khan and was one of the best swordsmen in his company.

"I asked him how he had come to be a monk. He said that during a battle, he had felt this overwhelming sense that all the violence and destruction was for no greater purpose. So, right in the middle of the battle he dropped his weapons and rode out of the fray up into the hills.

"He found a small pool of water. He dismounted and freed his horse. He stripped down and bathed himself in

It's Really More Simple Than That!

the pool-a sort of baptism if you will. After this he left everything behind, and naked, walked further into the hills to find his teacher.

"After a long time he came to a small compound where he knew he would find his teacher. There was a wooden gate at the front. There was a bark roof over the door to protect it from the rain. He was not let in because they said he was not ready. He knelt down in the Zen position and waited. He said that he waited for several days. He never moved from that spot. The hot sun beat down on him; the rain soaked him to the bone. Finally, a small, old monk came out and gave him a small wooden bowl with some broth.

"The monk took him in and nursed him back to health. It was there that he was taught the truth. After he learned what he could from them, he was turned out to roam the countryside to teach and to learn more.

It's Really More Simple Than That!

"He was teaching in a small village when the Khan's men rode in and destroyed everything. All of the men were killed; some of the women and children were captured and taken back to the camp. For some reason, he was saved even though he was in the center of it all helping with the injured. The Khan's men did not harm him but took him back to the Khan.

"Genghis Khan had watched him drop his weapons and ride off. So did many of the other men. For some unexplainable reason, he was not harmed. There was a strength that was within the monk that intrigued the Khan. It was for this reason that the Khan kept him by his side until he died. The monk taught the Khan many things about life and helped him over to the other side at his passing.

"The monk then roamed the countryside and came across a village that had been raped and pillaged while he

It's Really More Simple Than That!

was still a warrior with the Khan. The villagers soon recognized him and did not believe that he had become a changed man. They wanted revenge. They had a trial, but he was already considered guilty. He was sentenced to be executed.

"He was saddened that there was no love in the village. He understood that they would be angry with him, but there was no love between the villagers. He was taken to the center of the village for the execution. He knelt down in the Zen position. When he looked up into the executioner's eyes, he saw Unconditional Love coming from them. He knew then that everything would be all right.

"He said that when the blade came down, he could feel and hear it slice through his neck. At that moment, there was a beautiful white light that surrounded the whole area. At that moment he understood that all of the negative karma that he had gathered

It's Really More Simple Than That!

in that lifetime was released in one motion. With the executioner doing it with Unconditional Love, he was not tied to him in any way.

"This was truly a gift of Love. Now he was able to continue on his spiritual path unencumbered. And that is how he came to me. Part of his path was to teach me what he had learned. When he went back to the compound where he learned his lessons, he found no trace of them. It was as if the place had never existed!
"With this new teaching about Love, I started to talk about it. I reminded the other monks that this is what we needed to teach. They all began avoiding me. Finally, I was taken to my cell and given some bread and wine. They walled me in. And all my writings about Love sealed in with me.

"I ate the bread and drank the wine. I lay down on the table and a great light opened up. I was lifted up into

It's Really More Simple Than That!

this light. I wanted the others to see this event but realized that they would only see my limp body on the table. They did understand Love and were afraid.

"It was quite an experience. Now I teach."

It's Really More Simple Than That!

ON THE SUBJECT OF MASTERS

"Some people think that being a master is the final goal. This is partially true. Because when one is a Master in the truest sense, there is no more to learn because he or she is able to embody Unconditional Love wholly and completely."

"Are there any Masters on the earth plane at this time?" I asked.

"Yes."

"Are you a Master?"

"No. I am still on the path to becoming one. We all are on the path to become Masters. Some of us have gotten distracted for various reasons and some think they are already there. I don't know of any person-

It's Really More Simple Than That!

ally. I do know that there are some who are here to help others know what being a Master is, just like Jesus did when he was here. Interestingly, the ones who claim to be Masters are not Masters. For when a person claims to be one, the ego has taken the place of Unconditional Love and masked itself as the Truth."

"So these teachers who come to us as 'Masters' are really fooling everyone?"

"Mostly they are fooling themselves, because if people pay attention, they will garner any nuggets of truth that may be there and not be misled by the chaff. You know the expression, 'To separate the wheat from the chaff?'"

"So there are many teachers and few Masters."

"Exactly! Everyone you meet on any

It's Really More Simple Than That!

level has the potential of teaching you something, but only if you pay attention. Some of our teachers are here to teach us how to be, but there are also some teachers that are here to teach us how not to be. We are all teachers and students. We each have something to teach and something to learn from everyone in our lives. That's why we are here."

"All except you, right?"

"Did you hear me say that I was a Master?"

"No, but you said that the ones who claim to be are not, so I thought you might just be one because you said that you weren't."

"If I pay attention, there might be something I could learn from you!"

"What could I possibly teach you?"

It's Really More Simple Than That!

"If we already knew that, then that lesson would be done, wouldn't it?"

It's Really More Simple Than That!

THE CIRCLE OF LIFE

We walked along the street, and I wondered why people weren't staring at us. Further down we walked by a glass storefront and saw our reflection. I almost fell over when I saw us together. He still looked Italian, but his long robes were gone. All he had was an outfit of a tweed jacket, sweater and slacks, very much the professor. He noticed me watching him, and he said, "Wouldn't want to stick out now would we?" No, but when I looked back at him there were the robes again-neat trick.

We walked over to the hospital and went inside. I looked around at all of the people, patients, visitors, and medical personnel. I looked back at the priest, and he was wearing scrubs with a stethoscope around his neck! I looked down at myself, and I had on

It's Really More Simple Than That!

the same green pants and top sporting a stethoscope as well! I caught up to him and asked him, "What are we doing here?"

"Learning about life," he said as we rushed down the hall.

"This is where people go when they are sick," I said.

"Also true. Isn't that part of life?

"Yes, but..."

"You want to know more about 'The Truth.' It's all here," as he stretched his arms out in both directions, "birth, life, death. All of it, right here within these walls twenty-four hours a day."

We walked down to the morgue. It was a cold place because of the refrigeration for the bodies. We walked over to a table where a doctor was

It's Really More Simple Than That!

working on a body. As we got to the table, the doctor looked up and greeted us.
"Doctor," he said to each of us as naturally as if we were regulars and we replied in kind to him. I wondered how we were going to pull this off.

"The first bullet entered the body through the left lung and exited through the back. The second bullet entered his stomach and lodged in the spinal column at the sixth lumbar," the doctor droned on.

As he continued, I noticed a young man standing behind the doctor that could have passed for the dead man's twin. He looked very distressed, and I suddenly realized that this was the dead man's spirit! The priest went to him and took him aside. He talked to him a minute or two. The young man nodded and a great white light appeared and the two embraced. The young man was

It's Really More Simple Than That!

greeted by two angels and walked into the light together. As the light faded away, the priest came back to my side of the table. The doctor droned on.

"What just happened?" I whispered.

"You don't have to whisper, they are all dead here and the doctor can't hear us anyway," he replied. "Neal, the young man, was still hanging around his body because his death happened so fast, and he also didn't know where to go because he had had such a bad life. He was in the middle of a gang fight when he was struck down."

"I told him that it doesn't matter what he had done in his life. He still gets to go home to the Light."

From the autopsy, we moved over to one of the drawers. He pulled the handle and the cold slid out and surrounded me as the body came into

It's Really More Simple Than That!

view. He looked to be a man in his seventies.

"He was eighty-six when he died just this morning." He had read my mind again.

"Was he important? Should I know who this man was?" I asked.

"He wasn't famous if that's what you mean. He was very important to many people, both his family and many people throughout his entire life."

"How did he die?"

"A stroke finally did him in. Basically, he was tired. I saw him yesterday and he was just waiting for the last of his family to let him go. This man wanted to be a doctor back in high school. He even took four years of Latin and German and skipped grades to make it happen. At the university he

It's Really More Simple Than That!

was at the top of his class but the Depression came, and he had to work and support his family. He came back, and then the other war to end all wars broke out, and he quit again and became a fighter pilot. During the war, he fought well. He saved many lives and was awarded the Distinguished Flying Cross.

"When he returned, he was married with two boys and another on the way. He went back to school at night to get his MBA. He worked hard and took care of his family. At forty-two he had a major heart attack. He contracted diabetes, glaucoma, arthritis, and he still pushed on. His wife died of Alzheimer's, his mother and mother-in-law of cancer, and he took care of them all. He ended up with a life in health care in spite of not completing his schooling in the medical field.

It's Really More Simple Than That!

"He was sailing his boat until last year, and he volunteered for the fire department until a month before he came here. Why is this important? Here lies a man who in spite of his original dreams, made the most of life in all he did. He was a very loving husband and father and friend. He was always there for all who needed his help."

"He sounds like a saint," I said.

"No, he was a lover, although he would have told you he was just 'doing the right thing.' He looked at the world for all of its opportunities and accepted the challenges. He embraced life and taught many others to do the same."

"So, he gave up and died?"

"Absolutely not! He was tired. He worked hard, and he played hard.

It's Really More Simple Than That!

It was time for him to come home. We all have that choice. Come with me." He slid the drawer shut and started off down the hall.

We went up the stairs and down a hall then into a room with a middle-aged woman lying in the bed with her family all around. The feeling in the room was one of dread. Much grief. The priest went right up to the bed and greeted the family as if he had known them for a long time. He looked into the woman's eyes as he picked up her wrist and took her pulse. He smiled; she smiled weakly. I attempted to look at the dials and the equipment like I was making sure it was working properly. I was noticing this interaction between the two, and there was more than just pulse taking. She started out seeming so weak and near death. After awhile, the color started to re-

It's Really More Simple Than That!

turn to her cheeks. Her breath was more even and not labored. Finally, the priest put down her wrist and turned to the family and said that everything would be all right now. We turned and walked out of the room. A ways down the hall I asked him what he had done in there.

"That was a perfect example of free choice."

"How do you mean?"

"That woman had a terminal disease. There was nothing the doctors could do to help her, and her family had come to say good-bye. She was at a turning point in her life. She had felt that she was taken for granted by her family and that she was not loved. I just helped her see just how much love there was for her from her family, friends and, most of all, God.

It's Really More Simple Than That!

She didn't know that she could change her mind and be healthy again. I merely helped her to remember."

"Remember what?" I asked.

The priest gave me a strange look like I should already know the answer. He said, "I helped her remember that she is a child of God and that she has a choice to finish her work here or go home. I reminded her of her lessons that she chose before coming into this life and that she still has more to do to share her love and light. I asked her which she chose, and she wanted to stay. I simply helped her accept the Love and the Light to heal her. Of course, the doctors will take the credit for this incredible healing that they have accomplished with this woman."

It's Really More Simple Than That!

"Doesn't that bother you?" I asked.

He smiled and asked, "Which is more important, the credit or the healing? We have one more stop to make." We walked down another hall and right into the neonatal department where there were about twenty tiny babies in incubators with various tubes running to many machines. The priest went to one incubator in particular. He put on a pair of rubber gloves and reached inside with his right hand and cradled her head in his palm. She was so tiny, so fragile. There was an almost pasty bluish tinge about her. She did not look good. As the priest held her little head, I noticed her color begin to change to a warm pink hue. She smiled up at him, and I looked up to him and saw he was smiling down at her. I could feel the flow of Love coming

It's Really More Simple Than That!

from him. It was getting warmer in the room. I knew she was going to be all right. As we turned to leave, I noticed the name on her chart. It was Grace.

We were charging down the hall again, and he turned to me and said, "It is important to welcome these little ones into the world and remind them that we are all in this together. And that it is a blessing that they have come here to join us."

"Sort of thanking them for coming."

"Exactly!"

With that, we were out of the hospital and back in our other clothes. I was headed for the trees by the university and turned to ask him a question, but he had vanished.

It's Really More Simple Than That!

THE SECRETS OF LIFE

The priest took me to a clearing in the small glen by the university. There was a large, smooth, flat stone about two feet high in the center of the clearing. It felt warm to the touch from the sun. We sat on the stone and started the next lesson.

"These are the secrets of life," he said matter-of-factly.
"You never do anything that you do not want to do."
"You never make a wrong decision."
"There is only Love and fear and the illusion of that fear."
"Only the special people get to go into the light."

I looked at him like he was crazy. He said that I looked like a deer in

It's Really More Simple Than That!

headlights. "What are you talking about?" I said finally.
"The secrets of life," he said, "those oft-forgotten truths that help us to understand the world around us."

"Okay, what do you mean by, 'You never do anything that you don't want to do?'" I asked. "That's not true. There are lots of things that we don't want to do."

"Everything we do is by our choice," he said.

"How can you say that?"

He explained, "We can only make a choice based on the information that we have gathered through-out our lives. We choose to act or not based on that information, but, either way, it is our choice."

It's Really More Simple Than That!

I was trying to figure this one out when he continued. "You may think that you wouldn't like to clean out the horse stall, but you want the horse. You don't want to pay the price of a gallon of gas and yet you want to go places. When you start to look at the big picture, you will find that there is nothing that you do that is not your choice."

He was beginning to make sense. "But what about the man who pays to have the horse stall cleaned because he didn't want to do it himself?"

"He traded cash for labor. He chose to work at another task for cash and trade that cash with the person who cleaned the stall. He still cleaned the stall. Maybe the person who cleaned the stall chose to trade the cash for food because he knows someone who

It's Really More Simple Than That!

enjoys growing food."

"So the trading of goods and services is still choosing to do what we want."

"Exactly! Some people think that they are doing things that they don't want to do as if it is someone else's fault. When we begin to understand that it is all our choice, then we begin to take control of our own lives. We accept the responsibility of our path."

"What about you? You didn't want to get walled up in your cell, did you? How can you say you chose that?"

"I chose that because I stood up for what I believed. Getting walled up in the room was part of the path. That was my horse stall to shovel, and I'm still riding the horse!"

It's Really More Simple Than That!

"So you wanted to get walled up and lose your life?"

"First of all, I didn't lose my life. I'm here in front of you aren't I? Secondly, standing up for my path was more important than my own physical body. You see, when we truly accept the responsibility for our choices, we become empowered. When we accept this empowerment, we walk our path without fear."

"It comes down to that Love and fear thing doesn't it?"

"Bingo!" he shouted. I had never heard him say "bingo" before.

The sun was straight overhead, bright but not hot. It was warm and inviting. The stone bench had been collecting the sun's energy all morning just as it had for centuries. It felt good to sit here.

It's Really More Simple Than That!

"So what about the thing about never making a wrong decision?"

"We don't," he said matter-of-factly.
"As simple as that?" I replied.
"Yes."

"What's the catch?" He had hooked me again.

"There is no 'catch,' just an understanding."

"What about all of the unlucky people who feel that they have gotten themselves into bad situations because of using their 'free choice' and feel stuck?" I said, "Didn't they make wrong decisions?"
"Those people that feel stuck are choosing to feel that way. That is the path they choose."
"Nobody chooses to have an abusive relationship!" I shouted back and stopped myself short.

It's Really More Simple Than That!

He was looking into my eyes with a knowing that conveyed that I knew better than that. I didn't think I did. How can a person not feel that they chose wrong when the twenty-year relationship they had with their spouse was nothing but abuse. But then, why would anyone stay in that situation if it really was that bad? Free choice? How could that be? You make a choice like that and you are stuck. He's a priest; he should know that when you make a commitment like that, you are in it for good. Good, hmmm. Interesting term. One should be in it for good. But the vows say "for better or for worse." All of this took about a second.

He was watching me. "What could anyone learn from an abusive situation like that?" I finally asked.

"What can anyone learn from any

It's Really More Simple Than That!

situation? What do we learn IF we pay attention? Why do we get ourselves into situations like that?" He was shooting these questions at me and smiling that smile of his that tells me the answer is right under my nose.

"Okay, I know you want me to say it is more of that love stuff," I said finally. "But I don't buy it! What can anyone learn from that, to not make that choice again? That's too simple!" I was shouting again.

He just smiled.

"Why do they get themselves into the same situation over and over again?" He was beginning to really bug me. He was sitting on the stone bench letting me rant on and on, and he just smiled. I felt that I had him but really knew that I was just digging in deeper.

It's Really More Simple Than That!

"At the university, why do some students seem to breeze through while others have to repeat a class or two?" He was still smiling.

"Because some students pay attention and the others don't." He was smiling this broad smile of "see, it is right in front of your face but you don't get it either" look.

So, I told him, "It's a karma thing. If we don't get it the first time, then we have the opportunity to learn it again…and again…until we finally do get it. That's our graduation! Right?!"

"Close. Quite often the lesson comes back to us more strongly. It's like the donkey and the two by four. You may first have to get his attention."

"That feels awfully close to home," I replied.

It's Really More Simple Than That!

"You can only make a choice based on the information that you have gathered since your soul's creation. Nobody can do better than that," he said.

"Then why does it seem that some people do better than that?" I still didn't buy it.

"Some people pay better attention and therefore, have more information. Some people have been here more times than others. It is different for everyone, and it is the same for everyone."

"Just when I think I am beginning to understand, you throw me a curve ball. What are you saying, 'different for everyone and it is the same for everyone;' that doesn't make sense."
"Are you sure?" he asked. He hadn't moved from his spot all morning. I was pacing, sitting and

It's Really More Simple Than That!

pacing some more. I thought he said it is so simple. Why was this so confusing if it was supposed to be so simple?

The ground beneath my feet was soft, and the grass was still cool. I could hear a lone bird in the distance declaring his territory. The breeze felt good in the early afternoon sun. I was thinking.

He broke in, "If you think you're right, go with that." Oh, fine, now he says I may be right. What kind of teacher is this? I wanted answers!

"If I am right, then that cancels out the decision thing as one of the secrets of life," I said this... mostly with confidence.
He just smiled. This was really beginning to annoy me. Why wouldn't he just tell me and get it over with. Too easy, I guess. If we

It's Really More Simple Than That!

knock out that one, then do we have to knock out free choice? How could all of our choices be good? He was still smiling; he knew I was working this out.

"With every choice, you have an opportunity to choose Love or fear. That's it; there is nothing else. Nothing!" He was pretty emphatic about this.

"New lessons come with every choice as well," he added.

"Another opportunity to choose, right?" I added.
"Right. Every choice, another lesson, another opportunity to choose Love or fear." The priest rose on this statement as if to signal the end of the lesson for today.
I was ready to go until I remembered the last one of the "secrets."

It's Really More Simple Than That!

"What about the last secret? Only the special people get to go to the light. What's with that?"

He smiled again. "It's true, only the special people do get to go."

"How can that be? That goes against everything that we have been talking about!" I was almost shouting.

"Think about it. Think about all that you have learned up to now and see if there is any possible way that it could apply."

There he went again, making me think. It seemed that this one was contrary to the rest of the lessons. Before this, I felt that he was saying we were all children of God and that we all belong in the light. With this "secret," there is exclusion. We are somehow not worthy of God's Love. Back to

It's Really More Simple Than That!

the old "original sin" and unworthy worms of the earth crap. No offense to the worms.

"Remember that the truth is simple. Get out of your own way and see." He raised his hand and laid it on my head. All at once I was transported to a beautiful place. It was all white stone. There was a rectangular pool in front of me and to the right, three broad steps led up to a plaza of some sort. There were huge columns lining the way to a building ahead. There were no windows or doors that I could tell. I felt drawn to the wall. I was wearing a white sackcloth robe tied with a soft rope and nothing on my feet. To the right of me, out of the corner of my eye, a figure appeared. It was Jesus! I recognized him from other encounters. I went to get down and prostrate myself, but he put his hand on my chest and

It's Really More Simple Than That!

caught me half way down.
"No, my brother," he said. "You are not to bow down like that. We are brothers, and you need to remember who you are. You are Loved."

He took me to the wall. It was solid, very white and felt sandy to the touch. He took my hand and placed it on the wall. Immediately, my hand went right through and with a breath I was inside an extraordinary whiteness! A feeling of complete peace and Love permeated my very being. This feeling of perfect Love was supporting me. I became aware that this was who I am. I am Love. I am Light. My worldly existence is merely an opportunity to learn about and express Love more completely. We are also here to teach others on their path. Each of us has the opportunity and the responsibility to use all the Light

It's Really More Simple Than That!

and Love that comes to us. That is the thing we forget. We forget that we get to have all the Light there is! All of it! Not just a part because it has to go around to those who deserve it the most. All the Light, for each of His children. There are no qualifications other than we must remember who we are. Once we remember, we allow all the Love and Light there is to flow through us. That is what I was experiencing. It was perfect bliss. I was allowed to experience this for a while, but it was time for me to come back. I next found myself standing next to Jesus. I said that I could just stay in this place forever. He said, "No, you can't. You have too much work to do. You need to remember and help others to do the same. You see, it really is rather simple. It is not always easy. Go in peace, my brother." With that, I was standing next to

It's Really More Simple Than That!

the priest who, of course, was smiling that knowing smile of his.

"So, did you learn anything?" he asked.

"Oh yeah! You would not believe where I just was. Well, maybe you would," I exclaimed, "It was incredible!"

"Was it really incredible? Or was it believable and very extraordinary?" He asked, "Didn't it seem real to you?"

"Of course it did! Why do you ask that?"

"You said it was not credible. What part of it was not credible? So, what did you learn?" he asked.

"Okay, all of it was very real. It was the most wonderful expe-

It's Really More Simple Than That!

rience that I have ever had." I started to explain what had happened to me and the words could not express the experience in an adequate way. He just smiled. He knew I was beginning to get it. To finally get a glimpse of the big picture.

"What about the last 'secret' of life?" he asked. "Is it true or not?"

I thought for just a moment, then it was like a clap of thunder in my head. I said, "Only the special people get to go home because we are all special, all of us are children of God!" We all get to go!

The priest was beaming.

It's Really More Simple Than That!

WHAT DO I DO NOW?

"So, what do I do with this information?" I asked.

He smiled, "What do you want to do with it?"

"Aren't I supposed to take it and 'change the world'?"

"Do you really think you can 'change the world'?"

"I don't know."

"That's what I like, strong convictions! What happened to the passion?"

"I'm not sure my passion is to change the world."

"Maybe, maybe not. Perhaps

It's Really More Simple Than That!

using this information to change your own life would be a nice start. Or, would it be easier to try to change the world? We can only make changes in the outer if we make changes on the inner. All things grow from the inside. What do you want to do?"

"I want to help others."

"How about helping yourself first?"

"How do you mean?"

"Are you where you want to be?"

"Well, no."

"Then start by helping yourself. Do whatever you need to do to get on track and go from there. Life is a process. If you were done with this process, you would be off to other things. Teach by example first and others will come to you. They will want to know

It's Really More Simple Than That!

your 'secrets'."
"I don't know any 'secrets'."
"Of course not. But, when something works for someone, people think there must be some 'secret' that is helping them succeed. Then when people learn these 'secrets' they discount them for being too simple and throw them away, or worse, attack them because they are afraid."

"That sounds ridiculous!"

"Look at history; I'm sure you can find one or two examples."

"So, what I need to do is work on myself and let the others come to me?"

"Or not, it's your choice. That's about it. Accept that you need to allow yourself to change. Be gentle on yourself. Don't keep hanging on to your fear of not

It's Really More Simple Than That!

being loved. Stop driving with the emergency brake on! This is real life; there is no emergency, only love! It really is as simple as that!" He smiled that knowing smile of his, turned and quietly walked away down the path.

I never saw the priest after that.

It's Really More Simple Than That!

It's Really More Simple Than That!

If you would like to know...

Donald Hood is a hypnotherapist in the Chicago area. He has been certified for over twenty years with various organizations including the National Guild of Hypnotists, National Federation of Hypnotists and Hypnodyne Foundation.

He is president of the Association to Advance Ethical Hypnosis and past president of the Institute of Lightworkers Alliance.

He has taught at Waubonsee Community College and has written many articles on various subjects including hypnosis and spirituality. He has appeared on TV and also lectures and teaches around the country and Europe.

It's Really More Simple Than That!

It's Really More Simple Than That!

To contact Don, please...

E-mail donaldhood@gmail.com
www.donaldhood.org

Donald Hood
PO Box 4232
Wheaton, IL 60189-4232

Remember...

It's Really More Simple Than That!